Estate Sale, Antique Show Bargaining and Sales Techniques

PREFACE

You are probably wondering what this book is all about? It deals with buying and selling items, objects and merchandise for resale that is or isn't new. The items are new or used and therefore deserve a correct price. When a seller offers used merchandise at a show, sale, or market, the price isn't always firm. In fact, through bargaining, it is manipulated lower by the buyer, or higher by the seller until a compromise is reached. Sometimes no compromise is reached and there is no sale. This benefits no one. Commerce is based on moving merchandise "out the door." Resale bargaining is how this can be accomplished.

I grew up in San Diego and started bargaining with merchants in Tijuana, and Ensenada Mexico when our family went there in the 1950s. It seemed like a game back then. I was a pre-teen and I was after the usual junk: firecrackers, small daggers, chess sets, and guitars. Unfortunately I never bought the tacky black velvet paintings which I wish I had bought now. Those have become collector's items. The same type of merchandise had so many different prices depending on which store you entered. These prices were anything but firm. The more you complained or threatened to leave, the lower the price would go. It paid to look around at all the shops for the lowest price and then start the process of getting an even better deal. Anyone who didn't do that and paid full price was a sucker, and there were plenty of those around for the shop owners to fleece. NEVER PAY THE FIRST PRICE OFFEDRED BY THE SELLER, in a market situation where the price can be negotiated. That is only a starting point. The buyer needs to ask for a lower price. If you don't ask, you don't get.

My father though me a lesson when I was just 9 years old. We were visiting Ensenada in Baja and I was in love with a great, hand-carved chess set. The store looked quite nice and I was used to paying whatever the clerk quoted for something in a store back in the US. The chess set wasn't marked with a price. I asked the clerk "how much," and he quoted a price of $25. I started to reach for my wallet when my father stopped me. He wanted to haggle with the clerk. He wanted to bargain. They went back and forth and finally I was able to buy the chess set for $16, a savings of $9 from the first quoted price. This was my introduction to bargaining and getting something for less when a price sticker wasn't attached to the object in a foreign land. Because of that experience, and many more along the way for over 60 years, I decided to write this book to help people who aren't familiar with the concept of bargaining.

This book will take you step by step from both the buyers and sellers point of view to show you how it works. It shows what makes bargaining tick. It uses tried and true methods to get both buyer and seller the best possible price.

As a student at UC Berkeley in 1969 I started buying beautiful things cheaply and then selling them for a profit at The Alameda Penny Mart Flea Market and the Berkeley Flea Market. It was a way to have some extra pen money. The Lord knows you never have enough money when you're a student. I was no exception and I was mostly broke until I started buying and selling. By doing this I had enough money to finally buy a car and be able to ask someone out. Before that, I led a mostly lonely student life with a few, also penny less friends.

After graduating from Berkeley, I sold things I made or owned or wanted to get rid of at The Rose Bowl Flea Market in Pasadena Ca, one of the oldest flea markets in the west. When I lived in Hawaii, I sold bamboo bongs I made for the Pearl Harbor US. Navy sailors at the Tam Flea Market. They wanted a piece of Hawaii and I had a supply of fresh bamboo from the Linus Pauling

Jr. estate that I had permission to cut for free. Bamboo grows like a weed in Hawaii. When I got into picture tile making in the LA area, I sold those at the Ventura Wednesday Swap Meet. My starting price was always higher than what I expected to receive. I had to have somewhere to go with my price because just about everyone wants something for less.

When you are the seller, you want to squeeze as much profit as possible from your buyers without turning them off. The buyer needs to feel like he is getting a deal. There is a fine line to follow so that everyone is happy. There are certain rules of engagement that can be followed to make the experience good for both Seller and Buyer.

For the last 15 years, as Vice President of my wife's Estate Sale Company, I sold everything that was for sale in the Estate Homes of other people. The merchandise varied from art work to kitchen supplies. We had tools to antiques. Although we had very firm prices at the start of a sale, we made exceptions. Even when the prices were firm and fixed, the company had a duty to the client to milk every last drop of cash it could by having some wiggle room on the later days of the sale. Having an offer list was useful on the first day of an Estate Sale because the prices needed to be firm. The offer list showed that if someone was interested enough in an item, they could offer what they would reach into their pocket to pay because they didn't like the opening day price. As our Estate Sale progressed, we discounted to try to move it all out the door. The last day of a sale, we typically reduced prices to 50%, and after 11am would discount even further. Sometimes we would take a ridiculously low offer for anything left over near the end of those sales. That way we provided more money for our client and had less to pack for Charity.

Much of selling is based on the principal of what someone will actually pay for a used item. The amount is really what the market will bear. Market value is driven by desire and amount of product available. If everyone is selling rubber ducks, and the demand was only for several people, the value would be very low. If I have the only rubber duck, and several people wanted one, my ducks value will be higher. This is economics as the supply and demand can determine the price. It is through bargaining that the price becomes real.

It is important to remember that a resale item isn't new when you are selling or buying. You can't be charging or paying "new" prices on a used item, unless it is scarce and desirable. If I have an early Superman comic book, it is worth much more than the new price. That also goes for some artwork as well. When you have common fair trade items, like furniture, that is where you can't charge new prices or anywhere close. Used furniture, excluding antiques, needs to be offered for about 25% of new to start and then haggle it out to move it out.

I have seen many types of bargaining from all of the buying and selling. There are certain un-spoken rules of engagement from both the buyer and sellers point of view. Ways of coaxing the price up or down so that both people get almost what they want. Bargaining is really a compromise. It achieves the best possible result for both sides. They seem to have forgotten the art of that in the U.S. Congress these days. The attitude of "take it or leave it," doesn't work so well in resale.

Remember these words: YOU WILL NOT GO BROKE TAKING A PROFIT! This applies to people selling at shows and also in the Stock Market. Make sure that if you are a seller, that you are selling and not running your own personal museum. If you are hesitant to part with one of your objects when you have a buyer, you are running the museum. If your prices are always high, and people won't even attempt to bargain with you, you are running the museum. You may think a particular item is worth much more than what anyone would want to reach into their pocket and pay you for it, still running the museum. Try to remember that an object is only worth what anyone else values it for. Otherwise, you may see your overvalued stock grow and grow without making the needed sales. You have become a collector, or worse yet, a hoarder. That is the worst example of when you are running your own personal museum.

If you are buying, it should be for either fun, collecting, or to profit from by later selling. Collecting is fine as long as you know the boundaries of your collection. That means knowing what you are buying. Stamps or comic books for example, is collecting instead of just getting something that looks cool. If you are just buying things that look cool, with no plan at all, you may be a hoarder. Hoarders need more and more stuff. It can be a disease and you might wake up one morning realizing that you need more space for your stuff because there is nowhere to put anything new. Remember George Carlin's rant about stuff and more stuff? If this sounds like you, call an Estate Sale Company, seek help!

This book is designed to help with the tried and true practices I found out about bargaining in the 60 years along the way. Having been on both sides of selling and buying, this book will represent both points of view. I stress that these are my own findings and experiences which may be completely different than yours. Even though my wife will tell you that I have gotten into more trouble doing this, I am only trying to help! I do hope this book will at least give you more confidence in your ability to go out and sell or buy, and of course bargain!

Christopher Reutinger

TABLE OF CONTENTS:

1-Buying Dos and Don'ts

2-Sellers and Prices

3-What Price to Buy?

4-What Price to Sell?

5-The Starting Point

6-Body Language

7-Rules of Engagement

8-Walk Away

9-The Mutt and Jeff

10-Bulk Selling

11-Bait and Switch

12-Knowing When to Change

13-The Best Time to Buy Stock for Resale

14-Bargaining Summary

1-Buying Dos and Don'ts

Remember this most of all. Never pay the first price asked from a seller unless it is the first hour of the first day of an Estate Sale. I know from experience that those prices are very firm. If you like something at an Estate Sale on the first day, but don't like the price, ask for an offer sheet and leave an offer. You might be surprised when they call you the next day to sell it to you for your price. Or, take a chance and wait until the end of the last day of that sale. They will be interested in moving out everything at that point. You may not even need to bargain much at that time. It is always handy to know how to approach the sellers, asking for a discount.

Just like time, the water and wind wears down the hardest rocks. You need to become the water and wind in your bargaining. Don't be in a hurry to carve your best deal. There is a saying: "Everything comes to he who waits." By being patient and not in a hurry, you are in control. If you are in a hurry, you will get a quick deal that isn't as valuable. "Haste makes waste."

Be friendly, whether you are buyer or seller. Chat the person up a bit. As the saying goes: "Smile and be happy, and the whole world smiles with you." If you come off as a jerk, the seller may tell you to leave. I have been at sales where the seller was a jerk and it made me not want to deal at all with him. Even so, you might be able to re-amp him and make the seller want to give you a great deal. The same rules go for the seller. Be happy and friendly and you will have better dealings with your buyers. They will come back to you again and again. They will seek you out knowing you will give them a good bargain. If you are an old curmudgeon, and not friendly, you will scare away the buyers who want to give you their money. And that had better be the reason you are selling, to get the money. Otherwise, your museum will grow.

When I sold, I wanted to stand out from the other sellers. I always wore a Stetson hat. Remember the Broadway show "Gipsy?" One of the strippers sang a song called "Ya gotta have a gimmick." That is how she stood out from the other strippers so people would remember her. Wearing that Stetson hat gave me a look or brand if you will. Doing something like that will set you apart from all the other sellers. Just as Cal Worthington, the car salesman in Southern California, had a huge ten gallon cowboy hat, stood on his head to make all deals, and had a dog named Spot. (Spot was never the same creature, but sometimes a tiger.)

It made him different and vive la difference! He sold so many cars he was a regular on TV. Find your own look. Dress to impress! Make people remember you.

When buying, admire the object of your dreams. Let the seller know that you appreciate what he has on the block. He may be getting rid of something that he has had a long time and loves. He could be short of cash and only selling it to make the money he needs and not really want to sell it at all. Admire what he has for sale, but make not your love of it so strong or obvious that he thinks he can sell it to you for top dollar. Sounds like dating a bit, doesn't it? In those romantic situations, you can't wear your heart on your sleeve. You have to play your cards close to your chest so as not to be too obvious. If you are too obvious, just as it would be in the pursuit of a lover, the other person may lose interest or worse. You have become too easy to have! There has to be some mystery and a tad of coolness so the seller isn't sure if you will buy or not. It is a fine line to tread, and takes practice. Ask the seller, how much the item costs. The seller will respond and you can say," I really like this……but I'm trying to decide how much." At that point you can offer a tad below what you really want to pay. Then you have drawn a line in the sand from where the negotiation will commence. If you start by asking "What is your best price?" and they quote you their best price, you will insult them by wanting it for less after that. When that happened to me when I sold, I would say, "I just gave you my best price." My rule of thumb is if the seller's price is more than twice what I want to pay, it is time to start politely disengaging and walk away. Stay friendly with the seller. You may want something he has at a later date. If you are rude and blow him off, he will remember you and always have a "special price" for you, meaning much higher.

When bargaining, buyer or seller, rarely have your arms folded across your chest. That is a negative body language sign. Have your arms or hands behind your back or by your side as you might to calm a barking dog. In fact dispel all negativity completely. Speak softly but carry a bargaining stick. Appear as if you are open to anything. That is how it should start out in bargaining. Either buyer or seller can lower the boom, nautical term, later depending on how the rest of "the dance" goes. Just like dating again, you try to show your prince/princess side before any frogs appear. Try to show your best image before the sparks fly. Although it isn't a marriage, it has similarities. If you are married, you will understand. The point is, you aren't married to the person you are bargaining with. Things can go either way with less investment. That is why a prince/princess persona works well.

If the bargaining is going poorly, don't keep whipping that dead horse. If you are the buyer, don't be afraid to walk away from the deal. This is again a position of power. It shows the seller that you can take it or leave it. Maybe this object you want to buy just isn't for you. You may find the same object around the corner. If you decide later you will pay the buyers price, you can always come back later in the day. Even if the object may not be there, believe that you will find another. Stay positive and you will stay happy most of your life. You may even find the object next week for the price you want.

If you are the seller and the bargaining is going poorly, suggest politely, if they have been polite to you, that maybe this item isn't for them. Again, suggest politely that they might find it somewhere else for the price they want. If they won't leave and won't bargain, this is where I would give the "If a dollar is important to you, it is certainly important to me," speech. There are exceptions. One time I had a doll for sale for one dollar and the parents would only offer fifty cents. Their little girl wanted the doll and was crying when they refused to budge and started dragging her away. At that point, the dollar became unimportant to me. I nicely showed the parents how cheap they were by just giving the kid the doll. Any kind act like that will be remembered by anyone who witnesses it, just as a dog remembers who has given it food. It is also good Karma. Needless to say, I only do this with small items in that price range.

Make sure before you start bargaining that the buyer accepts the form of payment you can offer. If you only have checks and credit cards, and the seller only accepts cash, all your bargaining finesse won't matter. You are wasting his time and yours. If you don't have cash, which I always recommend having gobs of if you are the buyer, ask what forms of payment the seller accepts before you start bargaining. When bargaining, actually take out the cash and show it so that the seller can see it. That could help you in the long run. I have offered large sums of money for objects, but only after the seller saw the C notes, did he start to get real with me. You can also make it real in your dealings by just showing how serious you are with your CASH!

Trust your senses. By knowing what you want out of a deal, you will be in control. When you are in control, it is easier to be relaxed and bargain from a position of power.

2-Sellers and Prices

The best thing a Seller can do is have everything marked with a price tag. There may be some mystery to not having prices, but I feel that is just plain lazy. Having everything priced means you won't waste time with anyone who is unrealistic about your valuation. If your marked price is within their price range to bargain, you're in business! By not having anything marked, it may turn off a buyer. Some buyers are timid and aren't really into starting to bargain until they know the starting price. They will then have more confidence to bargain with a seller.

I know some sellers prefer not to price anything because they want to size up the buyer and offer him a "special price," meaning higher. They think they will get more this way. By looking at how well dressed the buyer is, the seller can figure out how much to charge. If you come to a sale dressed in fine clothes and shoes, you my friend WILL get the special price, a higher price! I find dressing in plain clothes, jeans with a shirt and inexpensive shoes can help your buying image so you won't be offered a high price.

If a buyer ever leaves his stall, as many do to look for bargains at the start of a sale, all business comes to a screeching halt when your merchandise isn't marked with a price. Most customers don't like waiting around while the assistant, or a friend in the next booth, stands there without a clue about what the seller wants and needs for his merchandise. I once waited 20 minutes for a seller, himself shopping at the show. He was a no show at his own booth. If all your wares are marked, the assistant/friend can do business at the same time you are finding bargains at the start of a sale.

Your marked price is just a starting point for the final price. My rule of thumb is to price the item at about twice the price I really want. A seller can always go down but can't go up (unless the buyer is really bugging him). In certain cases, I HAVE QUADRUPLED THE PRICE!!! Here is a real life example:

Buyer: "You give me best price"   The dish was marked at $20.
ME: After remembering I had payed $10 for this plate, I said "Ok…$15."
Buyer: I give you $10 dollar"
Me: "Wait, you asked for my best price and I gave it to you".
Buyer: "No, I give you $10 dollar"
Me: "Ok, let's start over. I tried to give you my best price. Now my best price is $30."
Buyer: "No I give you $10 dollar"
Me: "Ok, now my best price is $60."
Buyer: "What happen to $15 dollar?"
Me: "That was when we were younger."

    Even then, at that point, some people just don't get it. It frustrates me for a few seconds, at the actual moment, but then I start to feel sorry for them, if they would just go away! These broken record people are usually not from the USA. Their bargaining technique was developed outside of America. If everyone will remember this: As a seller, you don't really have to sell to anyone who is unreasonable. As a buyer, you really don't need to buy from anyone who is unreasonable. Stay in control of your situation. You have the right and the power to deal or not deal with anyone. Again, if you sense that they are being unreasonable, just take a deep breath and stop bargaining. Just walk away or ask them to walk away. It can be done very politely and you will feel better having done it.

But now, back to the point. In this same situation, had the buyer offered something higher than their starting point, I might have taken it. Or, I might have said again "If a dollar is important to you, you must know a dollar is also important to me. Give me $14." The point I am making as a seller is, you can always squeeze a tad more out of the deal. Selling the plate for $13 would have still given me a profit. But this buyer would only keep offering me the same price, their only price, their best offer not mine. By being indifferent to my first price, I don't want to reward them with it. They didn't like my "best price," so the bargaining continues from a different price. Their starting point was their only price. As they weren't bargaining, I decided not to bargain also and to jack up the price to get them to leave. They were dead wood and wasting my and their time. Unfortunately they didn't figure that out. Stay in a position of power at that point. Don't waste anyone's time, certainly not yours.

Your tagged price should be based in reality. An item really worth $50 and tagged for $200 won't sell. Items tagged this way will remain as part of your personal museum collection. Remember that you are there to sell, to move it out." Repacking," is the only dreaded word in the seller's vocabulary. Many buyers already know about what they should be paying if they are looking for a specific item. When they approach, as said in the end of the film Casablanca: "this could be the beginning of a beautiful relationship." This is where the misty magic starts in bargaining. The bare bones! By how much desire do you wish to sell this thing, complimented by how much desire the buyer really wants to buy it. This IS the time to look like Gary Cooper, or John Wayne. Remember, twitching is a sign of weakness… pilgrim. The hint of a smile. Both with bargaining guns at the ready, strapped to their legs.

3-What Price to Buy?

As stated before, and this book is about resale bargaining, everything you are buying or selling is used and was owned before. IT ISN"T NEW! You can't ask for a price as if it were new unless you want to add more items to your personal museum collection. I have found that asking for a price of around one third to one quarter of the new value helps to move out the stock. If you are buying for resale, it also means you have to pay less for it if you want to make any kind of profit. If you go buying something close to real market value, it needs to be something you really want to keep and not resell. Otherwise, you will have a hard time making any profit on that item.

From a buyers point of view and if you are buying for resale, you need to pay about half of what you intend to sell it for. Otherwise you are spinning your wheels. If you are just selling stuff you bought years ago, things you may have collected and just want to get it out of your hair, any price is WHAT THE MARKET WILL BEAR. You are liquidating and price isn't as important.

Sometimes objects you have bought years before may have increased in value. Here is an example. In the 70s, Bauer Ware and Catalina Island pottery started becoming the rage for California collectors. Bauer ring ware plates that once sold for $3-6 dollars started to climb. By the middle 80s to 90s these same plates were now selling for $40-60. Catalina Island pottery, the pieces fired on red/brown clay, not white, had an even more stellar climb. That clay was mined on Catalina and you were buying a tiny piece of the island. That reminds me of selling in Hawaii. The US. Sailors wanted to take home a small piece of Hawaii. Now, both Bauer and Catalina have cooled off a bit. Huge collections of each languish at Antique Shows and Estate Sales. The reason for the cooling, in my opinion, is there is a saturation of these collections at shows that were built piece by piece. The mystery of finding it piece by piece is gone. It seems common place to see a big collection at any show. The buyer has no idea how much time was involved in finding the collection one piece at a time. They don't know the collector built his collection over many years. By having a huge collection, all being there in one spot, it looks common place. I had a huge Catalina Collection that didn't move when it was all together. As a huge collection, it was only worth what the market would bear in bulk, what someone would reach into their pocket to pay for it. I changed strategy and started only bringing a few pieces to each sale. By doing that, I had made it rarer to find. I even got good prices with only a few units of Catalina Island Pottery. The funny thing is, the same customers kept coming back each week to buy whatever I had, and usually found something else to purchase from me as well. It drove the same buyers back to my stall each week. Having regular buyers is very important to survival when selling week to week.

Knowing the best price to pay becomes very important if you view selling as a business. There are online auction sites which you can subscribe to for the "gavel," out the door prices. This costs money! A free and easy resource is Ebay. I don't know of much that exists that isn't sold there. You need to find the margin on the left of the Ebay selling screen, the one marked "sold items." Ebay merchants may ask for high prices to start out in their auctions but that isn't what they actually sell for. You want to know how much a certain item ACTUALLY sold for to figure out how much you should pay for it. Now you will have an idea of what the market will bear when you find that item at a show. If you can't sell it for twice as much, it isn't as good a bet for resale. It may end up in your permanent museum collection. Again, the rule of thumb is to pay around half of what you can then sell it for or it may keep being repacked from show to show.

4- What Price to Sell?

Many sellers get wrapped up in their offered price for a specific item. They refuse to sell lower, and then continue to have more and more stock as they don't keep moving the merchandise out. This is where the beauty of bargaining comes in. As long as you are making a profit, anything goes. If I have offered to sell an object at several shows and it doesn't move, it should be considered overpriced. At that point, even a few dollars in profit is advisable. Try to stay "liquid" with your assets by discounting and moving it out. As a seller, you get to decide if your buyer will be happy, or Very Happy! I would go backward and forwards with making my buyers happy. If I made a killing on one item with someone, I might offer a "give it away" price on another just to keep that customer happy. By doing this, you will drive the same customers back to you again and again and you don't go broke taking that profit.

I have already mentioned that as a buyer, you can't show your hand about how much you want something. The "take it or leave it," cool, calm and collected attitude works best. Even if what you want to buy is the last piece you need to complete your collection, you can't show any excitement. Here is that Gary Cooper look again. If the seller even smells desire coming from the buyer, all the bargaining in the world won't help. Just like dating, you have become too easy to have. In that case, expect to pay close to the marked price.

By the same token, if you are selling and the buyer seems desperate to buy your item, don't bargain as much. You can move the price a tad lower to show good faith but be rather firm with your price. The buyer has signaled you that they must have it. You hold the all the cards now. Moving your price a tad in their favor will keep them interested, but only move a tad. Take advantage of their mistake.

We noted that most marked prices are just a starting point, a jumping off place from which bargaining will determine what the final price will be. If you have an unrealistic price marked on your object, again it might scare a serious buyer away. You need to be close to real market value with the starting price. As stated before, if you are just clearing out the garage, and don't care really how much you are paid, great. Take any offer later in the day after the "dealer buyer vampires" have left. But if you are a professional seller, profit is everything. Here is another example:

If I buy a plate for $10, I usually have it marked for sale for $20. If I buy a carving for $5, I would then have $10 marked on it. By pricing my items this way, I can remember what I paid for them and what I need to sell them for to make a profit. If I am offered $15. I can take that profit or try to squeeze one or a couple more dollars out of the buyer. Or I can decice that I have had this item for sale too long and discount it to move it out.

5-The Starting Point

When I am selling and a buyer makes an offer, it needs to be at least half of my price I have marked for me to even want to begin bargaining with them. If you have your prices marked at twice of what you paid, the buyer is offering you, with their offer, the price you paid for it. Your bargaining upward from there will produce how much profit you make. If they offer you less than half your price, lower than you paid, just smile and say no. It doesn't pay to try to bargain up from less than you paid. It is a lesson in futility and not much good will come from it.

From the buyers point, if you see something you want and even half price is too much for you, you can say certain things to find out if the seller will go lower. Admire the object and then say: "I really like this, and I don't want to offend you with this offer but…would you take?" Being polite and to the point is always good. Another great line is: "I really like this but I only have this much money for it". If I had a dollar for every time I heard that one, I wouldn't be writing this book! I would be retired in Baja. You may find a seller who is just liquidating his stock and may take your offer. It never hurts to ask. "If you don't ask, you don't get." Find out, like limbo, how low they will go!

My rule of thumb, as stated before, is to offer at least half the marked price for what I want to buy. You can always go up with your offer if it falls on deaf ears. If you ask a seller what is their "best price," you will then insult him by offering less than that. Remember the example: "I give you 10 dollar"! Only ask for his best price when all else fails; when he doesn't seem interesting in bargaining at all. If he then doesn't have a best price, he is a curator and sales groupie. He is at the show to hang out and be seen by his peers. He doesn't care about bargaining and it is time to walk away.

6-Body Language

One of my favorite buyers is Tom from Malibu. He is a big lovable, friendly guy and has deep pockets. I know when I see Tom that if my price is right, I will sell him lots of stuff. In fact, I have liquidated items to him he wasn't even interested in to begin with. He knew my price was "insane," and he just can't resist a great bargain. Carpets, art work, and other white elephant items, if offered to Tom for an unbelievable price, would move out of my stall. I didn't need to pack them up or take them home. I was grateful.

Tom employs a technique of silent bargaining with body language that is very effective. After he asks "how much?" he then frowns and slightly shakes his head "no" if he doesn't like your price. By his being silent and letting me do all the talking, he is now in the position of power. If I come down and lower my price to where he is happy, he smiles and shakes his head slightly "yes". I have adapted this technique from the seller's point of view. When the buyer offers a low price, slightly shake your head no, smile and don't speak. Now you have the power over the buyer. It puts all the pressure on the one talking to move the price. The silent one can remain firm until the price is right.

We have discussed how your arms should be. Having them crossed is negative. Even crossing them when you want a buyer to leave doesn't always work. Have your arms either behind your back or at your sides. Smile and be friendly. That's the way to make anyone want to deal with you. By being positive and friendly, you will have more repeat business, or make the sale to a new customer.

When a buyer asks you a question, if you are selling and sitting down, get off your butt. Stand up and go over to them. Try to be helpful and answer all of their questions. Don't look lazy! Show some interest to the prospective buyer. They are there to give you their money. If you stay seated, you aren't respecting that. If it looks like you don't give a damn about selling, it will turn a buyer off. To sum it up, by being friendly and attentive, you will get the sale and have more repeat business!

7-Rules of Engagement

Here is a practical example of a buyer and seller in the middle classic bargaining. The buyer collects old Mexican Hand-blown Glass from the 1950s. The seller has a large 1950 Mexican glass vase in cobalt. The seller doesn't have the piece priced.

Buyer: "What do you want for the blue vase?"

By not identifying the piece for what it is, he pretends to know nothing about it. It is just a nice blue vase. Not a bad tactic and it shows no emotional attachment. This is by contrast to saying "How much do you want for the 1950s Mexican Hand Blown

Glass Vase." Your seller doesn't need to be Sherlock Holmes to figure out that you are at this show looking for just that kind of merchandise. In that case, he will have a special price for you my friend, a higher price.

Seller: "I want to get $30. For it"
Buyer: "It's nice, but I don't know if I have $30 for it. Would you take $15 cash?"

A cash payment sometimes makes a difference in bargaining. It is always good to let the buyer know you have cash. Even so, after a real cash offer, the seller knows you ARE interested. As he doesn't know how much so, he may be slow to come down. By not having the vase marked to help him remember what he paid, he is just guessing at his profit margin.

Seller: "Well, I might do'er for $25."

Knowing that the seller did move down, but not a lot, the best tactic is to come up slowly, but not by much.

Buyer: "I might have $18 for it".

By saying this, the buyer has decided he can pay $20 and is angling to get there on the next round of bargaining.

Seller: "I can't take less than $22 for the vase".

The seller is putting on the brakes with that statement. You can believe him of not. I never let that statement stop me from continuing to bargain.

Buyer: "Split the difference with me. I'll give you $20 but that's my top."

Now the buyer has drawn a line in the sand and only over $2. At this point someone has to give or the deal is dead. This is where we find how much the seller wants to keep his stock over how much the buyer wants it. An experienced seller might come back with a compromise.

Seller: "You split the difference with me. Give me $21."

With the seller doing this, he makes the buyer look stupid if he walks away over one more dollar and the seller has milked a dollar more from the deal.

I was recently at an Estate Sale on the second day of the sale. I saw a garden statue that I liked and found the seller who could move the price up or down. The statue was offered at $35 dollars and being the second day of the sale, I offered $15. The seller came down to $25 and then wouldn't budge. I came up to $20, more than half the marked price. I even took the $20 bill out of my wallet to show him I had cash and was serious. The seller wouldn't budge or go lower. He didn't offer to split the difference with me, $22 or $23 dollars so I walked away. I guess he was the "close out buyer" and/or wanted the statue for himself. All I knew was, the statue is now still his problem. He has to pack it out or consign it. It was a nice statue but only an impulse buy for me. I was later happy that I walked away. I imagine that seller was conflicted and unhappy later that he didn't take advantage of a real live buyer with a cash offer. This example leads me to our next topic.

8-Walk Away

In the previous example, if the divide between the seller's price and the buyers offer is too great, as in $22 asked and $18 offered, that is the time for the buyer to walk away. He can say something such as: "I really like the vase, but not that much." By keeping the conversation open, he gives the seller another chance to come down. The seller, when he sees the buyer start to walk away, can say something like this: "Come back later in the day and if the vase is still here, I might do a tad better." Even if nothing is said by either after bargaining, the buyer should walk away. He can come back later in the day, preferably near closing time, to try to get the vase for less.

Walking away from a high price isn't a sign of weakness, it is a strength. It is also possible that the buyer might find the same vase the seller is offering in the next isle and for the buyer's starting price of $15. Sellers should remember that they are there to sell, not preside over the personal museum. How much packing do you want to do at the end of a show? It is always better to take a small profit on a few items instead of packing them back up for the next sale. This is especially true of items that are breakable. China, porcelain and fragile breakables fall into this category. If you ignore a small profit, and repack, it is possible your breakable item might not make it to the next venue in one piece. It would be wiser to take the profit, even if it is small, to insure you won't be the victim of a broken piece when you next unpack. That just equals a complete loss. I advise buyers who are buying for resale to stay away from easily breakable stock unless the profit margin is just too hard to resist.

9-The Mutt and Jeff

This technique of bargaining takes me back to the streets of Tijuana, Mexico in the 1950s. If only I had known enough to help my father when he was bargaining for my chess set. My older brother Marty wanted to buy a guitar from the plethora of guitars hanging in the many shops of Avenida de Revolution. I was with my brother and trying to help him. We would work as a team. We would try to execute the "Mutt and Jeff!" Marty found what looked like a great guitar except it had a $400 price tag on it. We knew from experience that the price had a lot of fat in it. Here is how the "Mutt and Jeff" works. It is like "good cop, bad cop." It is when 2 buyers gang up on the seller without the seller knowing what is happening. Marty was the good cop and I was the bad cop. I only played my roll when the bargaining reached an impasse.

Marty: "How much for the guitar mister?"
Seller: "For you, my friend, I have an especial deal! Half price, $200."

Marty: "The guitar is real nice, but not that nice."
Seller: "I will give you the friend of the mayor price, $150."
Marty: "That's still too much, I need the friend of the family discount!"
Seller: "Ok, I sell this to my family for $100."
Marty: "Aw gee, that still too much!"

At this point the seller doesn't go lower. It is now my turn to step into the action.
Me: "Come on Marty, I saw a guitar just like this, down the block for $40."
The seller shot me a stare that could have melted metal. I was in his way to make a killing from my brother. He was NOT pleased.

Me: "Come on Marty, I just KNOW we can get a better deal down the street."
Seller: "I will sell you this fine guitar for $50." He then looked at me like I was poison. I smiled back.
Me: "Aw Marty, come on. This guy wants too much for the guitar!"

The final outcome was, we got the guitar for $40. I had become a thorn in the seller's side with my wining and trying to drag my brother away. The shop keeper knew we had money and wanted to make a deal. He wanted to make the sale and a small profit. The last laugh was on us however. Crossing the border, the customs agent asked what we had purchased in Mexico. We showed him the beautiful guitar. He then said: "Those are real nice. The shopkeepers get them from central Mexico for around $12." The moral of this story is, in Mexico, the sellers won't sell you anything unless they are making a profit. Learn from this example.

Another example of the "Mutt and Jeff" is by using the cell phone as Jeff while you are alone and bargaining at a dealers stall. You don't even need to be talking to anyone, I KNOW! This is ruthless bargaining and you can spin you "other person" any way you want. It can be your partner or spouse or just a friend. It is like the TV show Millionaire, when they get a call to a friend. In this case, your friend is the naysayer bad cop and trying to convince you that the deal isn't good for you. You can be the good cop and ask this fictional advisor to look the object up and research the price on the computer, with of course negative results to the seller's merchandise. Here is an example:

Me: "How much is this old chair?"
Seller: "That chair is from the 1700s. It's an antique!"
Me: "Ok, how much is it?"
Seller: "That antique chair is $800."

I know the chair is an antique and French. Maybe it is from the French royal family and valuable. I haven't let on to the seller that I know diddly about it. All I am showing the seller is I am interested and it is just an old chair to me. His price is about what I think it would sell for in an antique shop, and we are at a swap meet.

Me: "How do I know it's antique and not a copy?"
Seller: "It's old French, can't you tell that. I don't sell reproductions."

The seller is starting to think he is wasting time with me. This is where I take out the phone and get into action with the "Mutt and Jeff."

Me: "I have a friend who is an antique dealer. Do you mind if I send him a photo and see what he thinks?"
Seller: "Go ahead."

At this point I use the cell phone's camera and take shots from different angles. I try to keep a straight face as I send the info into cyberspace to nobody.

Me: "This might take a while so if anyone else needs your help, go ahead and help them."
Seller: "Ok, I'll be interested to see what your friends thinks."

As I am not in a rush to try to obtain the chair, I am showing a "take it or leave it" attitude. The dealer knows I am interested if I am taking pictures to send out for advice, but he doesn't know how much. After a few minutes, I make a call to my fictional friend. I can now spin, within reason, the information any way I want.

Me: Hello, Charlie? Yah… you saw the pictures? What do you think for $800? … He wants way too much for the chair? What do

you think it is worth? You looked it up on your computer? Ok, I'll offer that but hang on for a sec, would ya?
Seller: "What does he think?"

    At this point, the seller has begun to question his price. I have sent pictures to an expert who is doubting the chair is worth $800. I am angling to get the chair for $400, half price. To do this I need to offer just below that at $375. I'm not sure the seller will let it go for that and I don't know his cost basis. You don't know until you ask, and if you don't ask, you don't get. What I do next is to blame my phone friend for anything negative. I just stay out of it at this point in a passive good cop role. I am there to offer the money but only following my expert friend's advice.

Me: "My friend likes the chair but thinks your price is out of line. He isn't sure it is original but he told me to offer you $375 cash."
Seller: "Well tell your friend he is out of line! I can't sell it to you for that. Can you do $500?"

    At this point, the fat in the seller's price has been shed. I can tell that he won't go much below $500 so I now must decide how much I want it. I decide that I do want the chair and adjust my bargaining to get it for $450. I don't want to offer that much to start, I can come up slowly.

Me: "Hey Charlie, He'll go $500. What do ya think? ... Still too much? Ok, but stay on the line."
Seller: "Look, $500 is as great price for the chair."
Me: "Charlie still isn't sure it's original. Would you take $400?"

By still casting doubt on the chair's origin. I can try to wedge the price lower. It is at this point that I take out four hundred dollar bills to let the seller see them. I want him to know he can have my money if I get a better price.

Seller: "I'll go $475. But that is it! I need to make some money on the deal and at that price, I'm not making much."

This is the moment of truth. I will come up to $450. And show the seller I have all of the money. If he doesn't go for it, not all is lost. I can come up to his $475 price and will have a chair worth $800 for that price, not a bad deal.

Me: "I'll go to $450, but I am paying more than my friend thinks I should."
Seller: "Look, split the difference with me, Take the chair for $465."

I know this seller and still want to do business with him in the future. He has come to this price on his own with my prodding. I will pay his price. We shake hands and I hand him $465 for the chair. On an object like an antique, if you can caste any doubt about it being a repro, with the help of your Phone-y friend, it can take a price down in a hurry. It doesn't work all of the time but does work some of the time.

10-Bulk Selling

If you have a lot of the same kind of merchandise, selling in bulk, even to another dealer, is a good way to rid yourself of more packing at the end of a show. I remember selling brass plates from Turkey. I had purchased scads of these plates, each with a unique design, dirt cheap at an Estate Sale. I was overloaded with beautiful etched brass plates. I had so many they looked as if you could find them anywhere. Because I had so many, it was like a collection and not something that had been put together piece by piece. It made them seem commonplace and there was only limited interest. I started to worry that I had bought these beautiful plates just because I liked them and maybe there was no real market for them at all. I found another dealer who liked the plates and if I made a few bucks on each plate, that was fine. I left some meat on the bone for the dealer. Make the money, take a profit in this case. Don't get too greedy or you might be left holding the bag, or brass plates in this case. Volume sales can move it out.

If you have a buyer who wants a discount if they buy 5 or more items in your booth, I find 10-20% is fair. This bulk discount avoids bargaining on every single item. The buyer will be happy not to do that also. It is just another reason to have EVERYTHING priced. If it isn't, this kind of bargaining really isn't possible as each item will have to have a starting price established that is bickered over. If the buyer wants a bulk discount on more than a few items, and you don't have prices marked, you will have this headache.

There have been times at a show, when I realize that everything I have has been seen over and over by the same buyers at that same market. Near the end of the day, I would cry out: "Bargain Sale, Every Thing is Half Off." By doing this massive sell off, I am getting back my original investment in my stock so I become liquid and be able to buy other items that might move more quickly. This kind of bulk selling is for survival.

11-Bait and Switch

When I am a seller, this buying tactic drives me crazy. The buyer comes up with 10 or more items and wants a bulk price. We bargain about how much, or I give them a percentage break, and we finally reach a deal. Or so I thought. The buyer now takes a few items away and wants to know how much for the rest. Again we bargain and reach a final amount. Then the buyer adds a few more items and asks, now how much? You can see where this is all going. Straight to last rung of the inferno for the seller. The buyer is wearing the seller down by changing the mix of items to be purchased. After getting a bulk price, in the case of taking already bargained merchandise out of the mix, the buyer is trying to get that same discount for much less merchandise. Sellers, beware of this tactic. I have even had very "cheeky" buyers then say "because I am buying so much from you, give me a further discount." That is double dipping from your profit margin. From my own experience, the people who bargain this way are usually from other countries. It may work for them there, but give me a home spun deal any day of the week. I have even asked buyers to leave when they start changing the mix from the first bulk discount agreed upon.

Here is an example:
Buyer: "I want these 10 things. How much you give me off?"
Seller: "I can discount them all for 10% off from the marked price."
Buyer: "That not good enough. I need better discount!"

Seller: "Ok, I will give you 20% off but not any more than that."
Buyer: "Ok, but I decide I don't want these 4 thing now."
Seller: "But I made my discount based on 10 items."
Buyer: "No, I want 20% off these 6."

    At this point, the seller needs to reset. He has given a discount based on selling 10 items, not 6. If you don't reset, you may sell at this discount for even fewer items than 6 as the buyer tweaks the assortment.
I usually just ask, in a nice way, for the seller to leave. I don't have to sell to anyone if I don't want to. I want to stay in control and in a position of power. Otherwise, the buyer has gotten everything he wants and I have given away merchandise for less than warrants.

    This same tactic was used at Estate Sales we ran on the first day of selling. These bulk scammers had the cashier frozen and were holding up the sale as others were in line behind them. I had to intervene and ask them to step away with what they were holding. Many times they would just walk away and leave their pile of stuff to be put back on the shelves. I made a mental note of these sellers and tried to keep them out of our future sales. They just don't get it. They are out for themselves, and if you are selling, you need to look out for yourself. If you encounter buyers who act this way, you have my permission to be unfriendly with them. If fact, if the buyer or seller is a jerk, "unfriend them." Life is too short to deal with these jackals.

12-Knowing When to Change

Knowing when to change your amount in bargaining will save a deal headed for a stalemate. This is again based on the desire each has to "get'er done," (thanks cable guy). You are the only person who knows when to do this. I can't tell you exactly, but I can give you a few examples:

If I am selling and don't have any emotional attachment to the merchandise, I may decide to move it out at a modest profit. Even a dollar profit will do if I have had the item for sale for a number of weeks. Again, by doing this, I get back my original investment with profit. I will agree to come down to that point to "move it out." This is extremely true when it is an item that is fragile and requires more attention to pack up. Broken stock is a total loss. Remember to try not to repack as much as possible.

If I am buying, and really want something, I am in control of coming up closer to the seller's price. I need to decide if I really want it or should walk away. In that case I agree to come upward if it is a rare and hard to find object. If this is something I have been searching for, for a long time, the price may not even matter. I would still try to hack a few bucks from the starting price. A buyer with money is a beautiful thing. If you are the seller, don't let them escape. Make sure to take their money.

Refunds for items sold isn't in your vocabulary. Buyers walk away and then get remorseful about their purchase. Somewhere in your stall, you need to have a sign you can point to that says "All Sales Are Final." This is something you must be firm with and should never change. If you are selling at a quality show, and you know the buyer and they are good customers, maybe then can offering a refund be worthwhile. Another possibility for giving a refund is if the buyer wants something of greater value and you will profit by it. This should happen on the same day the buyer bought the original item from you, not months later. Otherwise you are getting into the credit business. Remember, try not to give refunds at all.

Another reason of knowing how to change in selling is the use of the merchandise. Unusual items may have different uses or made up uses. I remember at the Berkeley Flea Market that I had 20 reflective cones that looked like large mixing bowls that I couldn't sell for 50 cents. All of a sudden I had a brain storm and put one on my head. I then yelled: "Space helmets, $2 each," and sold every last one! If you have a white elephant in your stock, can you invent a new use for it? Strange kitchen items come under this category. Invent a new use for your strange item. It helps to have great imagination doing this.

    I have seen some sellers who won't bargain. There price is final. They have nothing better to do than run their own personal museum and hold court over it. Being at the sale is a social deal for them as they most likely don't have much of a private social life. They won't change no matter how hard you try to get then to.

    I have seen some buyers who won't do anything but chant their low ball offer. They are just like sellers with only one price. This won't accomplish anything except wasting both people's time. Sellers, recognize when this is happening to you. Don't be so wrapped up in making any deal possible that you acquiesce to these turkeys. Buyers, if your seller won't bargain, just walk away.

You both can say things such as:
Seller: "This deal really isn't for you."
Buyer: "I guess you like owning this."
Seller: "I bet you can find it for less somewhere else."
Both: "Have a nice day!"

    Stop wasting your time with them. They will never get the point of bargaining. They will never change but you can by not taking part in this sort of nonsense. They are there for some other reason.

13-The Best Time to Buy Stock for Resale

There are two times when it is good to go looking for new stock. I remember my experiences of selling at a flea market or swap meet. When I would unpack, I was swarmed by other dealers in the early morning. If you are selling at a show or flea market, don't unpack until later in the day when the general admission people are starting to enter the venue. I only had other dealers as buyers early in the morning. They were intent on getting my new stock for rock bottom prices. What should this tell you? You need to become one of those dealers who is looking to buy at that early morning time. Try to get your new stock from someone who is selling as a "first timer." It is their first and only time at the show to sell items that they want to liquidate from their homes, garages, storage units, and barns. They have never been at this sale before and my never be seen again. They may not even care what price they get, just as long as they leave the show with nothing left. I remember buying a shoebox of broken watches for $20 from first timers which actually had a 14K gold wristwatch. I was able to sell the watch later in the same day for melt value: $200, ten times my investment. First timers are just cleaning up their clutter. They aren't involved in the daily bargaining that you are now subscribing to. Early morning is a great time to look for new stock.

    The second best time to shop is toward the close of a show. Pack up your merchandise and go looking for bargains an hour before the show ends. You may find a dealer who just wants to move everything for half off as I sometimes did. You may find something really special that a dealer has had a while and will deeply discount just to move it out. You may find a first timer who has just taken a box out of the truck that he forgot to display at the start of the show. You know he doesn't want to take anything home and therefore you can pick it up for a song. At the end of a show is also a great time to look.

14-Bargaining Summary

Whether you are Buyer or Seller, when you bargain with anyone, it helps to know what you really want out of the deal. It helps to show no emotion. No one needs to win or lose. By moving the starting price downward, it gets things done. If you don't ask, you don't get!

Always be friendly. Try to make some small talk as you would with a friend. I found that if a buyer made me laugh or smile, I usually gave them a better deal. This also works for the seller to amuse the buyer. You catch more flies with honey than you do with vinegar.

On the other hand, if the buyer or seller is a jerk, make the choice to not bargain with them. You can still try to be nice about it unless they aren't.

Try to have good body posture. When dealing with either buyer or seller, stand up straight. Keep your arms unfolded, at your sides or behind your back. Give the impression that you are happy and healthy. This is all done as a sign of respect to the other person before the bargaining begins.

Phrases for a buyer:

"I really like this but I only have (this much money) for it."
"I don't want to offend you but would you take…for it?"
""This is really nice! Would you take…cash for it?"

With that approach, try to show the cash to the seller. "How much is this?" (Don't identify or show any knowledge of what it is) Try silent bargaining after that.

In these examples, try to offer 50% less than the marked price. That should be your starting point. If 50% less is really still higher than you want to pay, try lower with the "I don't want to offend you…but."

"What is your best price?" (Use this only when a seller won't budge and only as a last resort)
"You're running a very nice museum here." (is a nice insult if the seller is a jerk and has treated you badly and won't bargain at all.)
"You must really like owing this." (Another nice insult)

Phrases for a Seller:

"I would love to sell it to you for that...but I can't."
"I have more than your offer invested in it."
"Come back later in the day and if it is still here, I might do a tad better."
"You know if a dollar is important to you, it's important to me also."
"Split the difference with me." (Trying to milk another few dollars out of the deal.)
"Maybe this just isn't for you." (Said when the buyer won't budge upward.)
"You might find this somewhere else for less." (When you want them to leave.)
"I would feel better if you pay me..." (Again, used to squeeze a dollar or two more out of the price)

Remember that if you don't have cash, be up front about it with the seller before you start bargaining. Identify what way you can pay for their merchandise. That way you won't be wasting his time or yours. If you are a seller, it is useful to have a swiper for a credit card as sometimes big ticket items can only be sold that way. The 4% charge for having one is nothing compared to making that huge sale.

Remember that the price marked is only a starting point. If there is no marked price, the first price quoted is the starting point. Sellers, it is better in my book to have everything marked so if you are away from your stall, things can get done. It also helps if a buyer wants a bulk discount by having the starting point from where you can discount you stock.

Mothers, don't let your seller children grow up to run museums. This is the first step to becoming the worst of the worst, a HORDER!

Fathers, don't let your buyer children grow up to pay full price. Paying retail is for tourists, or worse yet, SUCKERS.

Raise your children to be patient. Have them be in control of their bargaining. Give them the ability to not worry about time. Everything does come to he who waits including the best price. Become the wind and the water against the rocks. Time IS on your side.

www.ingramcontent.com/pod-product-compliance
Lightning Source LLC
Chambersburg PA
CBHW030055230526
45471CB00003B/1103